Stuff Every ——

# COOK

—— Should Know ——

Copyright © 2016 by Quirk Productions, Inc.

Library of Congress Cataloging in Publication Number: 2016930953

ISBN: 978-1-59474-936-0

Printed in China
Typeset in Goudy and Franklin Gothic

Illustrations by Kate Francis
Production management by John J. McGurk

Quirk Books
215 Church Street
Philadelphia, PA 19106
quirkbooks.com

10 9 8 7 6 5 4 3 2 1

The publisher and authors hereby disclaim any liability from any kitchen fiasco that may result from the use, proper or improper, of the information contained in this book. In other words: Exercise caution when operating a food processor. Don't run with knives. And never forget to keep your pantry stocked for three meals a day.

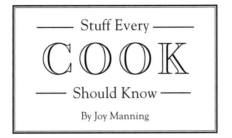

Stuff Every

# COOK

Should Know

By Joy Manning

QUIRK BOOKS

PHILADELPHIA

**To my niece, Henrietta.**
*I can't wait to teach you all this stuff cooks should know, and so much more.*

# Introduction

Learning to cook is not something that people do during the normal course of life anymore. Many grow into adults and have their own children without having acquired the skills needed to scramble an egg or boil spaghetti. Thankfully, a shift has occurred in recent years; everyone is more interested in food. In some cases the obsession translates to eating out more, but often a budding culinary enthusiast looks within. Wanting to cook is one of the best impulses that can wash over a person, but the path from desire to dinner is rarely a straight line. There is stuff every cook should know, and you'll find much of it in the pages that follow.

This book is a crash course in fundamental home cooking. These pages contain basic need-to-know information, like a chart for meat doneness temperatures, and outlines meant to help shape your own ideas, like a guide to throwing a dinner party. You won't learn everything you should know about home cooking here, but you'll learn a lot of essentials as well as how to direct continued self-study. Consider what you're about to read a starter toolbox that you will add to over time. Hopefully, reading this book is the start of a beautiful relationship between you and your kitchen.

# YOUR TOOLS

# Organizing Tips

Judging by the sheer number of charts, magazine articles, and online slide shows dedicated to the topic of organization, you'd think that keeping your kitchen in order is akin launching a spacecraft. The truth is that basic common sense plus an awareness of your own preferences and habits are your best tools for creating an organized kitchen. That said, keep these guidelines in mind as you stock and store all the things you need for the heart of your home.

- **Things that play together stay together.** Most household organization comes down to one simple idea: things that tend to get used together should always be stored together. For example, you should keep all baking cookware and equipment in the same cabinet or drawer. (Likewise, flours, sugar, baking soda, etc., should share the same shelf in the pantry.) That way, when baking day arrives you don't waste time hunting for the pie plates or cookie cutters. Apply this thinking kitchen-wide and you'll have what you want at your fingertips most of the time.

- **Use buckets and bins.** Forget fancy when it comes to kitchen storage. The simplest buckets, bins, baskets, and crocks make ideal silos for frequently used utensils such as spoons and spatulas. You can also neatly corral napkins, dishtowels, and silverware this way. Tuck the bins inside drawers or cabinets for easy storage and to . . .

- **Keep counters clear.** An open and inviting workspace will motivate you to cook. So after every kitchen session and especially before bedtime, remove clutter from countertops and put items back where they belong. Wipe down all surfaces and make sure nothing is in the sink.

- **Get a recipe binder.** In this digital age, it's still easier to work from recipes on paper, even if you found them online. Splashing olive oil on a printed-out recipe is no big deal (especially compared to your laptop), and you don't have to worry about fingering a pricey screen with greasy hands every time it fades to black. To prevent paper clutter, keep favorite recipes neatly stored in a binder for easy reference.

- *Mise en place.* This is a term professional chefs use; it means "put in place." It's the process of preparing, measuring, and organizing all your ingredients *before* you get to work, and it's a good way to make your cooking more foolproof. Having all the ingredients laid out beforehand increases the likelihood that every ingredient will actually make it into the dish.

# How to Work with a Small Kitchen

If you find yourself despairing over your kitchen's limited square footage, remember that many restaurant kitchens serve dozens of diners every night out of even tinier spaces than yours. In reality, you don't need much to turn out great food at home: a few basic pieces of equipment (a cutting board, a knife, a skillet, a pot), a small slice of countertop workspace, and a love of cooking.

- **Zone out.** Establishing specific work zones can make a small kitchen feel more organized and spacious. Mentally block out areas for storage, chopping and other food prep, cooking at the stove, and cleaning up after. Work inside the space dedicated to the task at hand.

- **Clean as you go.** Dirty dishes pile up fast in a small kitchen, so keeping things clean as you go ensures much-needed breathing room. Wash up, wipe your workspace, and put things away while you work. This is especially important for knives, which will stay sharper longer if they're not left sitting for hours with acidic foods stuck to them. Cleaning is part of successful cooking.

- **Ban unitaskers.** Kitchen gadgets are a lot of fun, but the truth is you don't need most of them. One big category of cooking tools that should never be permitted in your kitchen if space is at a premium: the unitasker. This is a piece of equipment that tackles one highly specialized job. Think of a strawberry huller, or a corn kernel remover. Both of those tasks are easier tackled with a paring knife. Before you acquire any new tool, ask yourself what you'll use it for. If you can think of just one thing, put it back on the shelf.

# Your Family Recipes

Family recipes are sacred, but many people don't realize this until it's too late—until they experience a bone-deep yearning for Grandma's apple dumplings and she's no longer around to make them. No one likes to think of a time when the elder cooks in the family won't be with us anymore, but one of the best ways to honor them and preserve their memory is to learn how to make their signature dishes.

Invite yourself over for cooking sessions with your loved one over the course of a month. Arrive equipped with:

- **Measuring tools and timers.** Many highly experienced home cooks haven't measured their ingredients or monitored a cooking time in decades.

- **A notebook.** Ask a lot of questions (What does the crust look like when it's done? Pale golden brown? Should I hear it sizzle?) and take detailed notes on the answers.

- **Your patience.** You'll need to ask sweetly to slow down and intervene in order to weigh and measure that flour or sugar, even if Grandma doesn't have to.

Learning beloved, time-worn recipes can be a painstaking process, but one day you'll be enormously glad you did it. And Grandma will be glad you asked. Well-documented family recipes can be a clan's most treasured heirlooms.

# How to Choose a Recipe

Recipes are like the syllabus for learning to cook. If you start with great source material, your kitchen prowess will grow each time you hit the stove. But if you work with a faulty plan—poorly written or untested recipes—you are likely to start calling yourself a bad cook and using that as an excuse to keep ordering pizza.

Once upon a time, most of the recipes in circulation were either handed down from one generation to the next or found in trustworthy sources like magazines, newspapers, and cookbooks—sources that had a strong incentive to make sure their recipes worked. Today, thanks to the Internet, recipes are everywhere. And most of them are terrible. Many either turn out tasting bad or just plain don't work.

When you understand how to cook, you can easily tell a great recipe from a flop just by reading it. But as you're still developing reliable recipe radar, use these tips for choosing a recipe.

1. **Find out if it's tested.** Some food magazines brag about their testing process. This is a good sign. For example, *Cook's Illustrated* has defined itself as a testing operation, and its recipes are virtually foolproof. When you shop for cookbooks, read the acknowledgments. If you see that the authors have thanked their recipe testers, proceed to the checkout with confidence. No testers mentioned? Put it back on the shelf.

2. **Check the comments.** You will continue to go to the Internet for recipes. That's okay. Read the comments for guidance. Are there hundreds, with many people saying specific things about their experience, maybe offering suggestions for improvements? Are the comments positive? Print that baby out and head to your kitchen with confidence.

3. **Read the recipe closely.** People who know how to write recipes always do certain things. Check to see if the ingredients are listed in the same order they appear in the instructions. And if an ingredient appears in one

section but not the other, it's a red flag. If the writer doesn't follow these basic rules, the recipe may not be one you can trust.

4. **Be honest with yourself.** Do you have or will you buy the ingredients the recipe calls for? Will you perform each step without improvising or taking shortcuts? If you don't intend to follow the recipe as written, put it aside. The best recipe is the one you will follow. After you've made a recipe successfully once, you'll have more freedom to experiment.

# The Difference between Stainless Steel and Aluminum

Walk into any kitchenwares shop or browse online for a simple skillet, and you are immediately flooded with choices. The most basic variable—and one of the most confusing—is the material that pots and pans are made from. You're likely to find seemingly similar pieces made from stainless steel, aluminum, and a combination of both. Each material has its benefits and disadvantages.

*Stainless steel* is a nonreactive metal, which means you can cook acidic foods in it, but it doesn't conduct heat as well as other metals. *Aluminum*, on the other hand, is a fantastic conductor of heat, which eliminates hot spots and makes even cooking easier, but it is reactive (not a good choice for tomato sauce!).

If versatility is your top priority, look for stainless steel cookware with an aluminum disk bottom, which combines the nonreactivity of stainless steel with the conductivity of aluminum. Higher-end cookware sometimes features a *copper* disk, which is even more conductive than aluminum. This type of pan is almost always dishwasher-safe another huge advantage. *Anodized aluminum* cookware undergoes a process that strengthens the metal and makes it nonreactive, like stainless, but typically is not dishwasher-safe.

Of course, these metals are not your only choices in cookware. Other materials you'll run across include copper, *cast iron*, and *carbon steel*. Those types all have specialized uses, but a skillet made from stainless steel or aluminum is most likely to be your everyday cooking workhorse.

# What Size Pot to Use

Recipes often are vague about what size pot you need to make a dish. If you are lucky, the instructions will specify if a vessel should be "small," "medium," or "large," but those terms are relative. As long as all the ingredients fit in your pot and you have some room to simmer and stir, everything will be just fine.

When choosing between a larger and smaller pot, bigger is safer—you don't want to deal with the mess of a pot of potatoes or pasta boiling over. That said, if the ingredients don't fill your pot at least halfway, the dish will probably cook faster than the recipe indicates. A larger-than-intended cooking vessel will increase the surface area, meaning that ingredients will be more exposed to the heat of the stovetop and evaporation will occur at a faster rate.

When you are shopping for pots, remember that for most home kitchens, four pots can tackle most jobs:

- **A 2-quart to 3-quart saucepan with a lid** for tasks like cooking rice, reheating leftovers, and steaming vegetables. This is truly an essential you'll find yourself reaching for every day. The ideal size for you may be a bit bigger or smaller than this range.

- **A 5-quart to 6-quart Dutch oven** for making braises, soups, and stews. Go for an enameled cast-iron Dutch oven if you can; the heavier material holds heat well, eliminating hot spots.

- **A 12-quart stockpot** for when you need to pull out the big guns. Think spaghetti night for the extended family or chili for Super Bowl Sunday.

- **A "butter warmer"** for when you want to melt butter for popcorn or any other reason. You'll also find yourself using it to reheat one portion of leftovers or to warm up all manner of sauces or gravy. These are not a standard size, usually less than 1 quart.

# How to Care for Cast Iron

If you ask experienced home cooks to name a cookware MVP, they are likely to talk about their cast iron skillet. This kitchen icon conducts and retains heat like no other and, if properly cared for, a single piece can last a century or more.

Some people are a bit intimidated by cast iron because of its reputation for being complicated to care for. And thought it's true cast iron does require a bit more TLC than stainless steel or aluminum cookware, it's hardly rocket science.

1. **Start with the seasoning.** Seasoning is the process of creating a tough film over the metal by lightly coating it with vegetable oil and then baking the empty pan upside down in a moderate oven (350°F) for about an hour.

2. **Keep it seasoned.** Though most cast iron pans come from the store already seasoned, it's still a good idea to repeat this process at

least once a year. You can fortify your seasoning by occasionally using the skillet to cook
something extra greasy, like a big batch of
bacon or fried chicken.

3. **Keep it clean.** You frequently hear that you
should never use dish soap to wash cast iron,
but that isn't true. Simply rinsing with water
is advisable, but when water alone doesn't get
the job done, it's okay to gently wash with
soap and water. Then rinse the pan promptly
and dry it thoroughly to prevent rust. For best
results, set the clean pan on a low burner until completely dry, and then rub lightly with
the barest film of canola oil before putting it
away.

# The Case for a Food Processor

Some people are resistant to investing in a food processor. These countertop appliances are expensive, costing between $100 and $250 on average. They are also heavy, bulky, and a bit annoying to clean. But these drawbacks fade as you grow accustomed to having this powerful machine in your kitchen. It can do everything a blender can do, and more. You might even pick up a second-hand model at a consignment store that has been barely used by its first owner.

With one, you can easily whip up plenty of foods that are expensive if store-bought: hummus, pesto, and nut butters top the list. These items are cheaper, healthier, and generally a lot better tasting when you make them yourself. Here are some other ways having a food processor will make your time in the kitchen easier:

- **Pizza and pasta dough** come together quickly and easily. The blades do all the kneading.

- **Chopping tons of vegetables** for produce-heavy recipes is much less of a chore when you don't have to do it by hand. Pulse the machine for the most evenly cut results.

- **Creamy soups** are basically impossible without a food processor or a blender. Puree all or part of a batch of soup for a thicker, velvety texture.

- Grind stale bread into **homemade bread crumbs** in just a minute.

- **Slicing potatoes** or other vegetables paper-thin is fast and flawless with the handy slicing blade. (And it's much safer than using a mandoline.)

- **Grated cheese** is not a chore when you use the grating blade. Buying whole blocks of cheese and grating them yourself saves money and tastes better, too (packaged grated cheese contains additives to keep it from clumping).

# How to Sharpen a Knife

Sharpening knives correctly is skill that can be harder to learn than cooking. The good news is you don't really have to learn how! The easiest way to keep blades sharp is to identify a knife sharpening service in your area and bring in your knives every other month or so for good sharpening. Kitchenware stores and farmers' markets often provide this service. Honing knives with a honing steel or ceramic rod between professional sharpenings (as pictured) will keep them sharper longer.

Another easy option is to buy an electric or manual knife sharpener. These devices hold the knife's blade at the proper angle so you get a sharp—not damaged—blade. Professional chefs and true aficionados use whetstones to sharpen their knives. Becoming proficient at this requires training and practice. YouTube how-to videos are a good reference if you decide to add "knife sharpener" to your résumé of special skills.

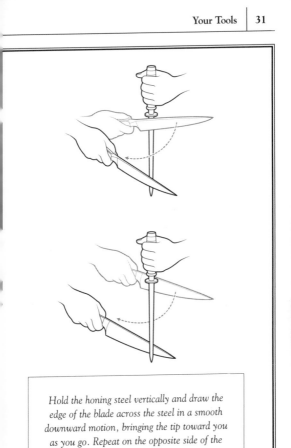

Hold the honing steel vertically and draw the edge of the blade across the steel in a smooth downward motion, bringing the tip toward you as you go. Repeat on the opposite side of the steel, honing the other side of the blade.

# Essential Knives

Gorgeous knife sets in handsome wood blocks can be tempting, but you really need only three knives in your home kitchen.

1. **The chef's knife.** This is the ultimate workhorse knife you will use daily for chopping meat and vegetables. Most models are between 8 and 12 inches long. Practice your chopping motion in the store to get a feel for the knife. If it hurts your hand, keep looking.

2. **The paring knife.** This sharp little knife is perfect for peeling and slicing. The shorter blade makes it easier to handle for detailed cutting jobs.

3. **The bread knife.** This long, serrated knife is a must for slicing baguettes, pizza, and other bread products. It's also the best option for slicing tomatoes and chopping chocolate.

# Basic Knife Cuts

Of all the cooking jargon out there, these terms, for the fundamental types of cuts, are what most home cooks need to know. Cutting ingredients properly is essential to good cooking. After all, if all your onion pieces are the same size, they will cook at the same rate. If not, some will end up overcooked and some underdone.

## Chop

This is the least precise word in the knife cuts vocabulary. It means using a knife to break down ingredients into smaller, more manageable pieces. The definition of "smaller" varies. This is a rustic cut and the one that is most often used in home cooking. Chopping isn't an exact science.

# Dice

Recipes will often mention a small, medium, or large dice. If no measurements are given, you can assume small means ¼-inch cubes, medium means ½-inch cubes, and large means ¾-inch cubes. And when the word *dice* is used, it implies even, straight sides. When dealing with irregularly shaped produce such as potatoes, you should square off the curved edges (saving the scraps for another use, such as making stock; see page 77) for perfectly uniform results.

# Mince

This word means to cut into pieces as small as your patience will bear—smaller than ¼ inch at the very least. Mince quickly by rocking your knife back and forth over the chopped ingredients until you are happy with the size. Mincing is usually done with a knife, but for an even easier option, you can usually save time by using a food processor (see page 28).

# Julienne

A culinary term that means cut into thin matchsticks, a julienne is best achieved by first cutting the item into thin, even planks and then cutting the planks into matchsticks. Most mandoline slicers have a julienne blade that can make quick work of this tedious cut.

# Chiffonade

Have you ever seen a scattering of pretty green confetti over a pasta dish at a restaurant? That's a chiffonade, which is chef-ese for "cut into thin ribbons." It's usually done to soft leafy ingredients such as basil. Stack leaves in a small, uniform pile on a cutting board and roll them into a cigar shape. Use your knife to thinly slice the roll into those cute green ribbons.

# How to Chop an Onion

Of all the things you take a knife to in your kitchen, the onion may be the most frequent guest on your cutting board. But thanks to its layered structure, chopping an onion can also be one of the quickest dinner prep chores.

*1. Peel the onion and trim both the stem and root ends, leaving enough of the root end intact so that the layers of the onion hold together.*

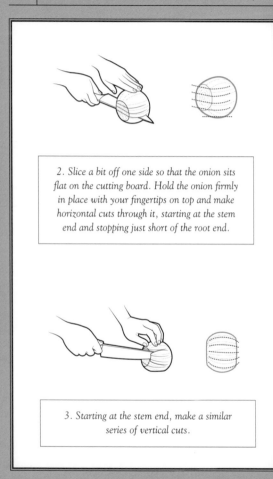

2. Slice a bit off one side so that the onion sits flat on the cutting board. Hold the onion firmly in place with your fingertips on top and make horizontal cuts through it, starting at the stem end and stopping just short of the root end.

3. Starting at the stem end, make a similar series of vertical cuts.

4. Finally, make thin slices at regular intervals
down to the root for a nice pile of evenly
chopped onion.

# How to Care for a Cutting Board

Cutting boards are commonly made of plastic or wood. Both are fine choices for your kitchen. Plastic boards are great because they don't require maintenance, and most can even be cleaned in the dishwasher. They do, however, tend to stain and scratch easily, and they aren't the most elegant-looking items. Meanwhile, wooden cutting boards are handsome and gentler on knives, but they require more care.

- **Wash and dry.** Promptly wash a wooden cutting board by hand each time you use it, and dry it immediately. (Never let a wooden cutting board soak—it can warp.)

- **Oil regularly.** Wooden boards should be oiled about once a month to keep stains, food odors, and bacteria at bay. With a soft cloth, spread a layer of mineral oil over the board. Let stand for two hours or up to overnight.

Then use a clean cloth to absorb excess oil and buff the surface.

- If you don't want to deal with oiling a tradi tional wooden cutting board, one good maintenance-free, plastic-free option is a wood-fiber laminate board. These are readily available online.

# Vinegar Can Clean Anything

Plain white vinegar is one of the best ways to clean your kitchen naturally.

- **Floors.** Add a few generous glugs of vinegar and a few drops of natural dish detergent to a bucket of hot water to get your kitchen floor spick and span.

- **Counters.** Fill a spray bottle with a mixture of 1 part vinegar to 1 part water. Use this solution to clean and disinfect your range and countertops.

- **Windows.** Straight vinegar is one of the best ways to get a streak-free shine on windows and other glass surfaces. Pour it in a spray bottle for easy use.

- **Dishwasher.** When your dishwasher gets a little funky, pour 1 cup vinegar into a bowl, place it upright in the top rack, and run the otherwise empty machine without soap.

- **Refrigerator.** Wash the shelves and drawers with a mixture of 1 part vinegar to 1 part water.

- **Automatic coffee machine.** Fill the water reservoir of the machine with a mixture of 1 part vinegar to 1 part water and let it run through a brewing cycle. It will help dissolve any mineral deposits inside the machine. When you're finished, run a couple brew cycles of plain water or rinse very thoroughly with water.

# YOUR
# INGREDIENTS

# All about Your Spice Rack

Having an arsenal of spices at your disposal can take even the most basic cooking to the next level. But what should you keep on hand when every recipe you bookmark calls for an obscure spice you can neither spell nor pronounce?

- **Start with the basics.** Before you try your luck with ras el hanout or Espelette pepper, establish your core spice pantry. Its precise makeup depends on your own tastes, but common essentials include cayenne pepper, cinnamon, cumin, curry powder, garlic powder, nutmeg, oregano, peppercorns, thyme, and smoked paprika. These ten cover a lot of culinary territory.

- **Explore geographically.** When you are ready to level up your spice game, expand using the flavor profiles specific to countries or regions. Like Asian flavors? Add Sichuan pepper and five-spice powder. Interested in Indian dishes? Go with turmeric and cardamom. Intrigued by the foods of the Middle East? Pick up Aleppo chili powder and za'atar. If you don't know where to start, visit the international cookbook section at your library. Most of those books will have a "pantry" section that can help you draft your spice shopping list.

- **Keep it fresh.** Remember that even the most flavorful spice will lose its zest as it sits in your cabinet. To avoid sprinkling your dishes with bland dust, buy spices in small quantities, and consider buying them whole: whole spices like nutmegs and cumin seeds keep much longer than ground powders, and you can grind just what you need for your recipe. Any ground spice you've had hanging around for a year or more should probably be tossed. Don't worry too much about the waste: As your cooking confidence grows, you'll learn which flavors you love best and center your spice rack around a few choice items that you always finish before they go flat.

# How to Season to Taste

The words "season to taste" mean that you should add salt a little bit at a time as you taste your dish. (It can also mean adding black pepper, a dash of hot sauce, or a splash of vinegar or lemon juice.) When the food tastes savory, full flavored, and just plain good, you've added enough salt. Over time, you won't fear these words, you'll know exactly what to do.

When you hear the judges on a cooking show complain that something is "underseasoned," what they mean is simple—this food needs salt. Too much salt (overseasoning) is a problem as well, but a much less common one among home cooks. Remember, though, that salt is easy to add and impossible to subtract. These pointers will help you season correctly every time.

1. **Don't be afraid of salt.** Certain foods such as beef, potatoes, tomatoes, and eggs are salt lovers; the amount of salt needed to make

them taste their best may seem excessive to newbies, because of the popular belief that salt is unhealthy. But more than 80 percent of the salt Americans consume is in packaged foods. If your diet is mostly home cooked, you probably don't need to worry about salt unless your doctor tells you to.

2. **Season before you cook.** Another stumbling block is when "season to taste" refers to a raw or partially cooked ingredient that isn't safe to eat (like pork chops), rendering the instruction useless. When seasoning raw meats, a good guideline is to use 1 teaspoon of salt per pound of meat. For dishes with ground meat, pinch off a small piece of the seasoned mixture and fry it up so you can taste it. Then add more salt, pepper, or other seasonings before you cook the whole batch.

3. **Salt the finished dish.** Let your palate be your guide. If you store salt in a small bowl instead of a shaker, you will eventually get a sense from feeling it between your fingers how much a particular food usually needs.

4. **Add acid.** Contrary to popular opinion, the most important seasoning after salt is not pepper but acid. A few drops of vinegar or a splash of lemon or lime juice can balance and brighten a dish immeasurably, even if it's not on the recipe's ingredients list.

# Cooking Oils 101

A lot of what you cook will include oil. Here are the major players and what you need to know to use them.

## Olive Oil

A bottle of inexpensive but quality olive oil (look for ones from Italy or Spain) is likely to be the most-used oil in your kitchen. It's the ideal fat for sizzling up the combination of onion, celery, and carrots that kicks off so many recipes, and it can double as an everyday salad oil, too. Look for bottles that say "pure olive oil" or simply "olive oil"—you don't need the extra-virgin stuff for most cooking tasks. Pure olive oil has a mild flavor that tastes good in most dishes.

# Extra-Virgin Olive Oil

An aromatic, green extra-virgin olive oil is a wonderful addition to your pantry, but it's expensive and not exactly a necessity. This kind of oil is known as a "finishing oil"; adding a drizzle to a bowl of soup or plate of pasta brings extra richness, aroma, and flavor. Cooking with it tends to destroy the more delicate flavor, so use regular olive oil for cooking and extra-virgin for plating or eating. Look for bottles with the words "first cold pressing" and a harvest date within the last year, which indicates freshness.

# Canola Oil

Next to plain olive oil, canola oil might be the second most popular among seasoned home cooks. Its neutral flavor makes it a good choice for baked goods, and it has a high smoke point, which makes it appropriate for frying. Canola oil is versatile, too, blending into a wide range of cuisines.

# Peanut Oil

Peanut oil, like canola, has a high smoke point and is great for frying, and its lightly nutty flavor makes it a natural match for Asian stir-fries. It also works well in certain nut-centric baking projects, including peanut butter cookies.

# Vegetable Oil

This is an oil made by chemically extracting oil from vegetables such as soy beans. It's also neutral in flavor with a high smoke point. It's cheaper than canola oil, but not typically as good in terms of quality or health benefits.

# How Long
# Stuff Keeps

Almost everything you buy at the supermarket has a sell-buy date, a best-by date, or both. But these dates aren't regulated; they're assigned by the manufacturer or seller, who want you to throw things away and buy more. As a result, they can be almost meaningless. Meanwhile, your nose has been tuned by millennia of evolution to tell if things are good to eat. You can usually trust it more than you can an expiration date, as long as you know what the food is supposed to smell and taste like.

You can learn to use your senses to tell when food has spoiled. For example, if you have an unopened container of yogurt that has been in your refrigerator longer than two weeks, open it. Does it look fresh (the same as new containers)? Any signs of mold or discoloration? Does it have a normal tangy smell? If so, take a small taste. Does it taste good? Excellent. This yogurt has not spoiled.

Here are some general guidelines for popular foods:

# Meat

Refrigerate for 2 days; freeze for 4 months. Meat that has gone bad smells terrible raw and even worse if you cook it. That said, meat, especially ground meat, is highly perishable and you should definitely move it to the freezer after 2 days in the refrigerator.

# Produce

Refrigerate most produce items for 1 week. Fresh produce that is stored carefully can often last for 2 weeks or more.

# Yogurt

Refrigerate for 2 weeks.

# Eggs

Refrigerate for 5 weeks. When in doubt, perform this simple test: Fill a bowl with cold water and add an egg. If it floats to the surface, it's gone bad.

# Milk

Refrigerate for 1 week. If ultrapasteurized, it will stay fresh longer.

# How to Reduce Waste

Once upon a time, high school students learned to combat waste in home economics courses, not to mention from their parents and grandparents. Today these skills are rare, and home cooks need to learn to minimize waste on their own. And there's good reason to work on this skill: the average household wastes up to 40 percent of its food. The good news is that much can be done to reduce and eliminate waste.

1. **Survey your pantry, refrigerator, and freezer.** Waste reduction begins even before you hit the grocery store. What items do you need to restock? What items do you need to use before they go bad?

2. **Make a meal plan.** Start the planning with anything you need to use up. (See page 86.)

3. **Go shopping.** Use your meal plan to make your grocery list, adding all the necessary

ingredients for dinner as well as the staples that make up your usual breakfasts and lunches. Shop exclusively from this list, avoiding tempting impulse buys.

4. **Prep ahead.** When you get home from the store over the weekend, make some time to prep for the week ahead. What can you chop in advance and set aside? Does the meal plan include soups, stews, or casseroles that you can make today? Remember, those kinds of dishes will only improve over a couple days in the refrigerator. If salad is on the menu, wash and chop the greens before storing in a salad sack or a plastic bag lined with a clean kitchen towel. Make your dressing right in a jar and put it in the refrigerator. An hour or so spent setting yourself up during the weekend will make weeknight dinners easier to pull together and dramatically reduce your food waste.

5. **Preserve it yourself.** Learning a few simple food preservation techniques can help you save foods before it's too late. For example:

+ Cooking chopped fruit with sugar and lemon juice until the mixture thickens yields a jamlike spread that lasts for ages in the freezer.

+ Pouring a salt water brine over green beans or carrot sticks and letting them stand, submerged, for a couple weeks at room temperature will yield long-lasting pickles.

+ Most herbs and leafy greens can be pureed with olive oil, garlic, and nuts for a tasty, freezable pesto.

+ If you want to get into canning, fermenting, pickle making, or other forms of traditional food preservation, many great books, classes, and online resources can teach you how. (Search online for "urban homesteading" for a wealth of resources.) You can prevent waste without them, but if they spark your interest, these skills are highly satisfying to learn.

# 10 Go-To Flavor Combinations

Recipes are somewhat like training wheels. As a novice home cook, you need them to get anywhere; but as your skills improve, you can ride without them. Though you absolutely can and should cook without recipes, it can help to have some favorite flavor combos in your back pocket to guide your inspiration. These versatile trios work with a wide variety of proteins, starches, and vegetables.

1. Tomatoes, basil, and extra-virgin olive oil

2. Scallions, ginger, and garlic

3. Plain yogurt, cucumber, and dill

4. Parsley, anchovy paste, and dried red pepper flakes

5. Lime juice, cilantro, and jalapeño pepper

6. Lemon zest, parsley, and shallot

7. Mustard, honey, and cayenne pepper

8. Watermelon, feta, and mint

9. Orange juice, green olives, and fennel

10. Chipotle pepper, oregano leaves, and cumin

# How to Start an Indoor Herb Garden

Having a little herb garden growing right in your kitchen is both pretty and practical. It saves you the premium you pay for herbs at the grocery store, and growing them yourself means you will have the freshest product possible. Follow these steps, and it can be easy, too. You'll earn your green thumb in no time.

- **Choose herbs that like to be inside.** Basil, chives, parsley, oregano, and thyme are all good options.

- **Pick the sunniest space.** Herbs need plenty of sunlight—five to six hours a day. Next to a south-facing window or under a skylight are your best bets.

- **Start with small plants, not seeds.** Starting seeds indoors can be tough. Just make sure your herbs are planted in quality potting soil in a container with good drainage.

- **Water daily, but just a small amount.** Add enough water to keep the soil moist—not wet. Many a kitchen herb garden has been lost to overzealous watering.

- **Harvest responsibly.** Trim herbs regularly, but don't go overboard. Each herb needs to be pruned in a specific way. Consult a gardening book or the Internet before picking up your shears.

# How to Conquer Your Fear of Baking

Most home cooks fall into one of two camps: the cooks and the bakers. Baking requires attention to detail, precision, and patience. Unlike a soup or stir-fry, you can't taste a cake during the preparation or correct flavors and texture as it comes together. This leaves many would-be bakers scared, but their fear is unfounded. Anyone can become a great baker if they want to learn.

- **Apprentice with a master.** Identify a person in your life whose baking skills you admire. Ask them to walk you through one of their favorite recipes in your kitchen. (And then make them dinner to say thanks.) Or sign up for a baking class. Hands-on learning and practice at the elbow of a pro is the fast track to overcoming your fear.

- **Self-study.** Visit a library or bookshop and spend time poring over the baking books. Take home your favorite and read it first—don't just venture right into the kitchen. Baking books often include technique instruction, and you will benefit from familiarizing yourself with those lessons before you start to bake. Cooking shows and YouTube tutorials also offer a world of education.

- **Start small.** Maybe you dream of baking your own wedding cake or creating a festive *bûche de Noël*. Before you attempt anything so grand, how about working on some brownies? When you get those right, perhaps try a basic pound cake. Tackling manageable projects first helps you build the skills and confidence you need for more ambitious creations later.

- **Practice, practice, practice.** Take to your kitchen frequently and with gusto. When recipes go wrong, try again until you get it right. Only through failures and repetition will you get really good at baking.

- **Stick to a scale.** Precision measuring is the surest path to successful baked goods. For this reason, many excellent recipes list weights in addition to volume measurements. Flour measured with a standard measuring cup can vary in weight from 3½ to 5 ounces. That's a huge difference! A digital kitchen scale, on the other hand, gets it exactly right every time.

# How to Measure Ingredients

In the United States, we cook a bit differently than they do in the rest of the world. We use finicky volume-based measurements (teaspoon, cup, etc.) for dry ingredients instead of the foolproof system of metric weights used by home cooks in other countries.

This is starting to change. You may notice more and more cookbook authors and food bloggers including weights in grams in their recipes in addition to volume measurements, especially when precision really matters, as in baking. You should invest in a digital scale for your kitchen and use these recipes whenever you can; recipes written this way are harder to mess up. You can also annotate your favorite recipes with weights as you make them so you can reproduce and alter them more easily later.

But until the dreamy utopia of weight-based measures comes to our shores, we are left mostly with recipes that rely on those old cups and spoons. To minimize measurement errors while scooping and pouring, keep these guidelines in mind.

## The Dry Goods

When measuring powdery ingredients such as flour, sugar, and baking powder, let this be your mantra: *scoop and sweep.* This method involves gently dipping your measuring cup or spoon into the flour (without compressing it) and then using the flat edge of a butter knife to level the top.

## The Wet Works

Liquid ingredients should have their own set of cups. They should be clear, labeled so that you can see the amount from outside the cup, and have a spout for pouring. It is possible to use dry cups for measuring liquids (such as water, eggs, or milk) but you need to fill them to the very brim for accuracy. That's hard to do without making a mess.

# The Sticky Stuff

What about peanut butter or honey? Anything that will stick mightily to the inside of the cup should be measured with an adjustable measuring cup. These have a movable plunger bottom that forces every last bit out of the cup and into your mixing bowl.

# Common Doneness Tests

Cooking meat to just the right level of doneness can be a bit tricky. Using a thermometer is the easiest and most accurate way to gauge meat's doneness, but many cooks prefer to judge by the way it feels. "The touch test" involves pressing the meat as it cooks and comparing it to certain areas of your hand or face.

## The Hand Test

Open your hand with the palm facing up and relax your hand. Press gently on the flesh at the base of your thumb, between your thumb and forefinger. That's what raw meat feels like. Lightly press together the tips of your pinky finger and thumb, and touch the base of your thumb again. That's well done. Repeating this move with your ring finger will show you how medium doneness feels. The middle finger to thumb tip will feel like medium rare. The index finger to thumb tip feels like rare.

## The Face Test

Relax your face and touch your cheek to see what rare feels like. The tip of your chin represents medium, and your forehead feels like well done.

## Baking Tests

The most common test for doneness involves inserting a toothpick or skewer into the middle of the baked good. If it comes out clean or with just a few moist crumbs, your treat is likely finished baking. With bread, gently tap on the bottom of the loaf. It should sound hollow.

# Meat Temperature Guide

Undercooking meat, especially ground meat, can lead to food-borne illness from contaminants like salmonella and E. coli. But if you overcook a good steak, it becomes dry and tasteless. Using a meat thermometer can save you from these fates.

Below are the minimum temperatures recommended by the USDA. In most cases you'll want to cook the meat to just that temperature and no further.

| Food | Temperature |
| --- | --- |
| Ground meat | 160°F |
| Beef and lamb | 145°F |
| Poultry | 165°F |
| Pork and ham | 145°F |
| Fish | 145°F |

# A Few Cuts of Meat

Most people rely on a handful of cuts for their everyday cooking. Sure, you might want a crown roast for a holiday feast, but the following cuts are among the most popular for weeknight meals.

## Chicken Thighs

Pound for pound, this is the most useful cut of meat in your butcher's case. Thighs are more flavorful than chicken breasts, and the dark meat resists overcooking. They are excellent sautéed, grilled, broiled, and braised. Thighs take well to marinades and seasoning blends. Buy them in bulk to get the best price; they store perfectly in the freezer.

# Chicken Breasts

One of the most popular items at the supermarket, these are healthy, versatile, and mild in flavor. A quick cooking method, either sautéing or poaching, prevents the delicate meat from drying out.

# Rib Eye

For special occasions and steak nights, a well-marbled rib eye is hard to beat. This cut has great texture and concentrated, beefy flavor. Season it generously and sear it on the grill.

# Skirt Steak

Less expensive than other choice steaks, a skirt steak is perfect for tacos or fajitas. Just remember to slice it across the grain for maximum tenderness.

# Pork Shoulder

Also known as pork butt or Boston butt, this large cut features plenty of flavorful fat and shines most brightly in a slow-and-low braise in the oven or a slow cooker. The meat becomes tender and shreds easily—perfect for pulled pork sanwiches and tacos. It always yields plenty of leftovers; stash them in the freezer for convenient dinners down the line.

# Pork Tenderloin

Low in fat and quick in cooking, pork tenderloin is the MVP of the healthy weeknight meal. It's mild and takes well to a huge variety of seasonings, salsa, and sauces.

# Ground Meat

Whenever possible, ask your market's butcher to grind meat from the specific cut you want. Meat ground to order will taste fresher than packaged ground meat, and you'll know exactly what cut you're getting. Always keep a pound or two of ground beef, pork, or turkey in your freezer for emergency stir-fries, meatloaf, and meatballs. Ground meat won't last as long in the fridge as whole cuts will, so use it or freeze it within one or two days.

# How to Save Scraps for Stock

Of course you can buy stock or broth from the grocery store. But wouldn't it be better to make them for free from kitchen scraps?

Note: You might need more salt than is called for in a soup you make with homemade stock, but don't be afraid to add it. You'll still end up with less sodium than if you used the store-bought kind, in which sodium is used as both a flavoring and a preservative.

## Chicken Stock

The most common kind of cooking stock is made from chicken bones, but you don't have to buy them at the butcher counter. Whether you're roasting your own bird or making the most of a rotisserie chicken, save the carcass in a big freezer bag, adding spare wings or other bones after your meals. Once you've got enough to fill roughly three-quarters of a large pot, put the frozen parts in the pot and add just enough water to cover. Simmer on low heat, partially covered, for a few hours. Strain for rich and golden homemade chicken stock.

# Vegetable Broth

Is vegetable broth more your thing? Save trimmings such as carrot peels, onion skins, mushroom stems, leek tops and ends, green bean tips, and corn cobs and freeze them until you have enough to fill up three-quarters of a stock pot. Omit cruciferous veggies (broccoli, cabbage, brussels sprouts, etc.), which will give your broth an off smell. Cover with water, simmer for 30 minutes, strain, and store.

# How to Stop Onions from Making You Cry

Onion is a key ingredient in many, if not most, recipes. But what if their fumes burn your eyes until you're crying into your dinner? Try these options to find out what helps make your kitchen a tear-free zone.

- **Keep 'em cold.** Storing onions in the refrigerator or freezing them for 15 minutes before chopping will inhibit those compounds that can be so irritating to your eyes.

- **Wear goggles.** This is not the most stylish option, but putting a physical barrier between your face and the food is a reliable way to stop those water works.

- **Get some air.** Chopping near an open window or under an exhaust vent will help disperse the chemicals and keep them out of your eyes.

- **Use a food processor.** After a quick rough chop, toss the onions in the machine and pulse until they are minced. The lid contains the fumes and the blade makes the job fast—two good ways to minimize the tears.

- **Give it a soak.** Trim and peel the onion, and then dunk it in a cold water bath for about 15 minutes. The water may draw out some of the offending compounds, making the chopping process easier on the eyes. One caveat: This method also tends to leach a bit of that oniony bite, leaving you with a bit less flavor.

# Common Conversions

One of cooking's best-kept secrets is that it can involve a surprising amount of math. For example, what if you want to double or halve your favorite recipe? You may find yourself going online to figure out how to convert measurements so you can scale a recipe to your particular serving needs. You can't commit all possible conversions to memory, but here are a few basic ones you should know.

| Volume Measurements | |
| --- | --- |
| 4 quarts | 1 gallon |
| 2 pints | 1 quart |
| 2 cups | 1 pint |
| 1 cup | 8 fluid ounces |
| 4 tablespoons | ¼ cup |
| 2 tablespoons | 1 ounce |
| 3 teaspoons | 1 tablespoon |

| Baking | | |
|---|---|---|
| 1 stick butter | 8 tablespoons | 4 ounces |
| 1 cup chocolate chips | 6 ounces | |
| Heavy cream | Whipping cream | |
| 1 egg | 1 tablespoon yolk, 2 tablespoons white | |

| Cooking | |
|---|---|
| 1 garlic clove | ½ teaspoon minced |
| Juice of 1 lemon | ¼ cup |
| 1 bunch scallions | 1 cup chopped |
| 1 medium onion | 1 cup chopped |

# Common Substitutions

Sometimes you want to make something on the fly but find yourself lacking one critical ingredient. Or maybe you want to cut the fat in a favorite dish. Knowing which kitchen staples can stand in for others gives you more flexibility when you cook. Here are some of the most common swaps, all of which you can substitute 1:1.

| Replace this | with this |
| --- | --- |
| Oil or butter | Applesauce (reduces fat) |
| Buttermilk | Yogurt (or yogurt thinned with water) |
| Ground beef | Ground turkey |
| Lemon juice | Vinegar |
| Tahini | Peanut butter |
| Mayonnaise or sour cream | Greek-style yogurt |

# THREE MEALS
# A DAY

# Mastering Meal Planning

Eating well and sticking to a budget are easiest when you have a weekly meal plan to guide you. Choose one day a week to do your grocery shopping, and always create the meal plan as part of your preparation for hitting the store. Before you gather your shopping bags and pick up the car keys, conduct a brief strategy session. You need only about 20 minutes, and when you're done you'll have a meal plan and shopping list. Just follow these easy steps.

1. **Review the contents of the fridge, freezer, and pantry.** Make a mental note of anything that ought to be used up in the next couple days. Note what leftovers or ingredients you have stashed away that could be the basis of next week's dinners.

2. **Get inspired.** Take a peek at your favorite recipe sources: pages you've ripped out of

magazines, new or favorite cookbooks, blogs and websites. Is there a new recipe you want to try? Do you have time one day this week to take on a new culinary project?

3. **Flip through past meal plans.** Eventually you'll have plenty of them, which you can store on paper or in an electronic calendar. See if there's anything you'd like to make again.

4. **Consult your family.** Negotiate with your spouse/roommates/family members about what sounds good—try as best you can to anticipate cravings. Is it too cold to have salad for dinner? Are you sick of chicken? What irrational whims or aversions can you foresee for the coming week?

5. **Fill the calendar.** Label each day with its dinner, scheduling more perishable stuff toward the beginning of the week and freezer and pantry fodder at the end.

6. **Make a list.** Compare the recipes' ingredients lists to your inventory and make a shopping

list. In addition to dinner ingredients, you'll also want to add breakfast, lunch, and pantry staples. Organize your list in categories based on the layout of your grocery store and your normal route through it. For example, the entrance to most grocery stores is near the produce section, so list fruits and vegetables first.

7. **Shop.** Buy only what is on the list. No impulse buys! Having a list is a good start, but sticking to it requires determination and practice. Something you buy on a whim can derail your plan, cost you extra cash, and increase your odds of food waste. If you really want it, you'll remember to work it into your plan next week.

# Solutions for Common Disasters

Before you panic about some culinary mishap, remember: Your kitchen is not the ER. Cooking is not a life-or-death situation (usually). It's just dinner, and you can always call for pizza. That said, you certainly may feel you're dealing with a full-blown catastrophe when something goes wrong. You feel frustrated, powerless, or, worst of all, like you will never be a good cook. That isn't true—every accomplished cook has many tales of recipes gone awry. Making mistakes is an integral part of the process of learning how to cook.

Not every kitchen disaster can be remedied. If your toast burns to a crisp, just throw it away. But plenty of times, dinner can be saved. Here are a few simple solutions to the most common mishaps.

## Lumpy Gravy

Pour gravy into your blender and puree until smooth again. No blender? Use a wooden spoon to force the gravy through a fine-mesh strainer.

## Cake Stuck to the Pan

Try freezing the cake and pan for several hours. Often this firms the cake enough that it can be removed without breaking apart. If that doesn't work or the cake is already broken, mix the pieces with icing and make cake pops or truffles, or layer them with whipped cream and jam to make an English trifle.

## Oversalted Food

It can happen fast—one minute your dish needs a bit more salt and the next you've gone too far. If you're making a soup, stew, or chili, adding an unsalted, bland ingredient (such as a grated potato or sodium-free canned beans) can even things out. Adding a salt-free liquid, like home-made broth, is another option. In other cases, try chopping the too-salty element and mixing it with unsalted ingredients. You may end up with something more akin to a chopped salad or homey casserole than you had planned, but at least it will be edible. Alternatively, if your cookie recipe calls for ½ teaspoon of salt and you mistakenly add a tablespoon instead, you're going to have to toss it. Don't throw good ingredients after bad.

## Jam That Didn't Set

When making fruit jams, knowing just the right moment to take your mixture off the heat is a skill that comes with practice. If you get the timing wrong, you may end up with a runny mess incapable of being spread on toast. Instead of seeing the result as failed jam, think of it as a successful sauce. Now you have a new condiment to drizzle on yogurt and pancakes.

# Overcooked Vegetables

Most people don't enjoy mushy broccoli or disintegrating asparagus. If your vegetables are too soft after too much time spent in the steamer or oven, don't fret—add chicken or vegetable stock, throw it all in the blender, and make a soup. A splash of cream added after blending is a nice touch. Serve with croutons or bacon bits for maximum I-did-this-on-purpose effect.

# Too Much Spice

Even for those who love to feel the burn, sometimes too much of a good thing is just too much. An overenthusiastic addition of hot sauce, cayenne, red pepper flakes, or fresh chilies can make dinner hazardous in a hurry. Try adding something creamy to cut the heat. Heavy cream, sour cream, and coconut milk all work well, but yogurt is the queen of cooling ingredients. You can sometimes balance heat with a few pinches of sugar, too.

# A Plan for Breakfast

You've probably heard that breakfast is the most important meal of the day. And though recent research suggests that old chestnut may be less ironclad than once thought, plenty of evidence suggests you should still eat it. People who start their day with a meal tend to weigh less than those who don't, for example. But as with most things in life, if you don't have a game plan for the morning meal, it probably won't go the way you want. You may find yourself grabbing a fast-food sandwich on your way to work or eating all the donuts in the lobby before lunch. Let these principles help you break the fast right.

- **You don't have to reinvent the wheel.** Eating the same thing for breakfast every day, whether it's a smoothie, a bowl of oatmeal, a couple fried eggs, toaster waffles topped with peanut butter, or whatever, is perfectly okay. In fact, some nutrition experts recommend automating certain meals (usually breakfast and lunch) so you don't have to decide what to have every day. Make sure the items you need for your regular breakfasts are always on your shopping list.

- **Make it ahead.** Love omelets but not the time it takes to whip one up every morning? Cook a big batch of your favorite omelet in muffin tins over the weekend and enjoy single-serving portions of protein all week.

- **Switch it up.** Some people thrive on breakfast repetition—but you may not be one of them. If you know that you prefer variety, make sure to have options at your fingertips. Consider items with a long shelf life, like yogurt and cereal. Frozen berries can stand in for more perishable fresh fruits and jazz up oatmeal, smoothies, and yogurt.

- **Keep it simple.** The easier it is for you to eat breakfast, the more likely you are to do it. There is nothing wrong with a simple slice of toast topped with peanut butter or cottage cheese or a couple hard-boiled eggs. Even a handful of nuts is reasonably nutritious and better than nothing if your tummy is growling. Store them someplace handy so that you can grab and go in a jiffy.

- **Rethink standard fare.** You know what makes a convenient breakfast? Last night's leftovers. A square of vegetable lasagna or slice of meatloaf tastes just as good in the morning as it does at night, and there's no law that says you have to start the day with cereal and milk.

- **Overnight your oats.** If you are an oatmeal aficionado, you almost certainly prefer the nutty, chewy, satisfying bite of steel-cut oats to old-fashioned rolled oats. But the long cooking time—about 45 minutes—probably prevents you from enjoying them on weekday mornings. There's a fix for that: Before bedtime, combine 1 cup steel-cut oats with 3 cups water in a pot. Bring to a boil, cover, and remove from heat. Let mixture stand at room temperature overnight. In the morning, pour in milk to taste, simmer for 5 minutes, and let stand off heat for another

5 minutes. Top with your usual fixings and enjoy.

An even faster way to have an oatmeal breakfast is to fill a jar with old-fashioned rolled oats and plenty of water and/or milk. It should look soupy—the oats absorb a lot of water overnight. Then stir in whatever you like. Nut butters, yogurt, cinnamon, and dried fruits are all good choices. Refrigerate the jar overnight, and in the morning, just grab it and a spoon and go. This style of overnight oats is eaten cold.

# How to Pack a Lunch

The most important factor in whether you will or will not pack a lunch is your level of commitment to planning. To help increase your odds of eating healthier and likely saving some money, you'll need to add lunch-friendly items to your grocery list and brainstorm items that you'll want to eat.

The most successful lunch packers do a bit of food preparation over the weekend so that they can quickly and easily pull together a midday meal on hectic weekday mornings.

- **Gather inspiration.** You might well like ham sandwiches, but you probably won't like them for weeks on end. Same goes for salads in mason jars, lettuce and turkey rolls, and avocado halves stuffed with tuna. You want a deep bench of lunch options to stave off boredom. Look to the Internet—and your coworkers' lunch boxes—to get inspired.

- **Consider your environment.** To some extent, your work or school space dictates the kinds of packed lunches you can bring. Do you have access to a toaster oven? Refrigerator? Microwave? Full kitchen? Think about where you will be storing, preparing, and eating your lunch.

- **Use your leftovers.** Leftovers are a natural for lunch. When cooking something that is lunch box friendly, double it. Don't forget that lunch offers the opportunity for transformation. Last night's roast chicken breasts plus mayo and celery equals tomorrow's chicken salad sandwich.

- **Gear up.** Get appropriate containers for the foods you like to pack. Salad fans and those who like raw vegetable sticks, for example, should invest in some small containers to hold the dressings and dipping sauces that make those lunches a treat. If you don't have access to a refrigerator, an insulated bag and small ice packs are key.

- **Heed your thirst.** Sure, you can probably get water in your workplace, but wouldn't a bottle of lemon-flavored sparkling water, lemonade, or iced herbal tea be a lot nicer? Pack yourself a great drink. It elevates the brought-lunch experience.

- **Don't forget treats.** You are probably packing a lunch to save money and be healthy. Still, include a small treat as a reward for meeting your goal. It could be a square of dark chocolate or some farmers market fruit. A little dessert goes a long way to making packed lunch more appealing.

# How to Balance Your Diet

Everyone wants to eat well-rounded and nutritious foods, and luckily you don't have to be a registered dietician to get the variety of vitamins, minerals, antioxidants, fiber, and other substances your body needs. Here are some great first steps.

- **Cut back on processed foods.** Choosing minimally processed foods the majority of the time will take you most of the way toward a balanced diet.

- **Eat more vegetables.** For most people, a balanced diet comes down to one main thing: eating more vegetables. And in the vast majority of cases, we mean *a lot* more. The recommended amount is four to five cups of vegetables per day. Vegetables have most of the stuff—fiber in particular—that you may be missing. Set a goal to eat them three times a day, at breakfast, lunch, and dinner, even just a small serving. Or if you just cannot deal with morning veggies, add a snack like carrot sticks to your lunch. Change your attitude so that no meal seems complete without vegetables. Two things can make it dramatically easier: stocking your freezer with a variety of frozen vegetables, which can be ready in minutes with very little prep, and keeping bagged salad greens in your crisper.

- **Eat more fish.** Most people don't eat nearly the recommended amount of fish, the main source of omega-3 fatty acids. The American Heart Association suggests you eat fish twice a week.

# How to Make Meals Ahead

Cooking ahead is probably *the* number one secret among busy people who manage to enjoy home-cooked meals most of the time. In fact, if you are a single person or living in a two-career family, it is pretty much the only option. Few people get home from a long day of work in the mood to tackle serious cooking. But if you get in the habit of managing your meals, it will become second nature. This skill is also likely to be a point of pride and the envy of your friends.

- **Carve out a block of time.** Two to three hours should do it. Obviously, scheduling this time for your day off is a good idea. Kitchen duty can be relaxing and rewarding, doubling as real quality time with your partner or kids. If you are single, enlisting a friend can make it much more fun. Even if you do end up on your own, try listening to podcasts, audiobooks, or music while you cook.

- **Know what can be cooked ahead.** In restaurant kitchens, cooks begin preparing some dish components well in advance of dinner service, leaving other ingredients to be cooked "à la minute," or at the last minute. Steal this strategy by figuring what you can cook in advance and what is best saved for later. For example, if you'd like a salad topped with fried eggs for dinner next week, make your dressing and chop your vegetables over the weekend, but fry those eggs right before you eat. Let common sense guide you.

- **Choose meals that improve with time.** Many recipes are famous for tasting better after a couple days in the fridge. Soups, stews, chilis, and braises form part of the better-the-next-day club. Often these dishes lend themselves to large batches, which can be frozen in single-serving containers for meals on the fly.

- **Use ingredients more than once.** Think about meal components that you can make over the weekend and use in several ways. If you roast and shred a pork shoulder, for example, you are halfway to quite a few quick-fix suppers. A pot of whole grains, like brown rice or quinoa, can become part of a wide variety of bowls with the addition of canned beans, cheese, salsa, or diced avocado.

- **Roast two chickens.** Roast chicken is the perfect Sunday supper—nourishing, comforting, and familiar. And if you have one bird in the oven, you might as well be cooking two. Leftovers are easy to use in sandwiches and salads and freeze perfectly, too. Use the carcass for homemade broth (see page 77).

- **Stock up on frozen vegetables.** Shake up last night's leftovers by adding a different side. Frozen vegetables are better quality than most people think and steam up almost instantly in a microwave. Have a spare half hour? Roast them in a hot oven with olive oil, salt, and pepper.

# How to Cook Frugally

Most home cooks confront a time when the food budget gets tight. In times like these, employ tried-and-true strategies to stretch a dollar at the grocery store and make it through to payday.

- **Quit packaged foods.** Whole-food ingredients aren't breaking your budget. It's the cookies and crackers, sauces and dips, frozen meals, and ice cream bars that are bleeding your wallet dry. Swear them off and you'll have more cash for things that really count (like meat and vegetables). You'll probably end up with healthier habits, too.

- **Go meatless or meat-light.** Meat, especially good-quality meat, should be the most expensive item on your grocery list. So to save money, you should buy less of it, but don't skimp on quality. Do so by planning a couple vegetarian meals per week and think of meat as a condiment rather than the center-piece of your plate. Round out your meal with legumes, whole grains, and vegetables.

- **Live on legumes.** The ultimate shorthand for cooking on a budget is when someone tells you they were "living on rice and beans." That isn't just a turn of phrase. Rice and beans is a dirt-cheap, delicious, nutritious staple of food-savvy people who have lived through lean times. Look to South America and the American South for the tastiest reci-pe variations on this theme.

- **Bulk up.** The best value inside most upscale or natural foods grocery stores is found in the bulk food aisle. That's where you can fill your own containers (or the plastic bags provided) with grains, dried beans, nuts, seeds, pasta, and other staples. These are often sold at a steep discount compared to the same items sold under brand-name packaging. Another approach to bulk shopping is to join a mem-bership-only warehouse store. Membership usually pays for itself in the savings you accumulate with savvy shopping. Keep in mind that this is a good option only if you have plenty of storage space and are committed to avoiding the waste that can accompany bulk packages.

- **Cook seasonally.** Even when your budget is constrained, don't skimp on vegetables. Look online for a chart showing what's currently in season in your region, and shop for those items. You'll always pay a premium for tomatoes in winter, for example, but they can usually be bought for a reasonable price in summertime. Usually you can save by buying directly from growers at a farmers market. Ask if discounted "seconds" are available. These are fruits and vegetables that are too small, irregularly shaped, or otherwise cosmetically flawed to sell for full price, but they taste just as great as the picture-perfect specimens.

- **Cook down your kitchen.** Most people have far more food on hand than they realize. Think about the odds and ends stuffed in your freezer, refrigerator, and pantry. You can whip up amazing meals from this forgotten stuff when you allow no other alternative. Challenge yourself to cook down the refrigerator, pantry, or the whole kitchen by skipping the grocery store for a week (or more) and relying only on what's on hand. You'll surprise yourself with creative combinations and save money in the process.

- **Plant a garden.** Nothing's cheaper than food you grow yourself. Seeds are an almost negligible expense, and seed-saving neighbors can help you get started for free. Sure, the project will cost you some time, but most avid gardeners relish the hours spent digging in the dirt. When harvest time comes, you can slash your grocery bill by more than half by "shopping" the produce section in your own backyard. Learning how to preserve your home-grown bounty will stretch your savings through the rest of the year. Even without a yard, a few containers for growing fresh herbs on a windowsill can stop you from buying those tiny, expensive packs at the grocery store.

- **Plan around sales and coupons.** Stop recycling that grocery store circular that gets dropped on your doorstep. Read it instead. You'll learn about the sales happening that week and which grocery items are most deeply discounted. Plan your weekly menu around the things you can get for a low price. You'll find coupons here as well. There's no shame in clipping them, but you can also find coupon websites and apps that take the scissors out of couponing.

# What to Cook When You're Sick

Whether you like it or not, cooking is the bed-rock of taking care of yourself, and there's no time when it's more important than when you're sick.

Unfortunately, there's also no time when you feel less like making yourself a meal. The average person gets two to three colds every year. With that fact in mind, prepare for flu season by making chicken soup in advance and storing it in the freezer for when you need it. For best results, leave out the noodles (they get mushy in the freezer) and cook them just before serving. Also important to keep on hand:

- **High-quality store-bought broth or bouillon.** Having a ready supply of soup-making liquid makes whipping up a pot easy enough to tackle even when you have the sniffles.

- **Eggs.** When you are all souped out, reach for eggs. Most people always have a few on hand, they are nutritious and satisfying, and most important, they take only minutes to make.

- **Jam.** Sometimes buttered toast with nice jam, alongside a soothing cup of tea, is just what the doctor ordered.

# The Benefits of Family Meals

Many of today's adults grew up in households where shared family supper was not the norm. This may be the result of kids' schedules being packed with after-school activities or jobs that keep parents tethered to their desks well past dinnertime. But research shows that family dinners convey an astounding array of benefits, including:

- Healthier body weight

- Improved self-esteem

- Reduced risk of teen pregnancy

- Reduced risk of depression

- Reduced risk of eating disorders

- Better grades in school

Intramural soccer kind of pales in comparison, doesn't it? And while the thought of producing family dinner most nights can be daunting, the payoff is considerable. No one is suggesting that your meals must be gourmet or elaborate. The simplest fare (meatloaf, grilled cheese and tomato soup, spaghetti and meatballs, roast chicken) gets the same results as recipes torn from fancy food magazines. Even the occasional take-out pizza is okay as long as it helps to gather the family together at the end of the day to relax over a shared meal and conversation. For best results, ban screen time for this one crucial hour of the day. Connection (not necessarily cooking) is the key.

# How to Cook for Children

Americans commonly underestimate the variety of foods kids are willing to eat—serving them frozen chicken nuggets, bland mac and cheese, hot dogs, and the like. In much of the rest of the world, kids eat exactly what adults eat, in smaller portions, and little fuss is made over it. Although some children (and adults) are frustratingly picky about what they'll eat, most are game to try new foods.

Still, remember that kids' palates can be more sensitive than adults'. So when cooking for young ones, think about how to adapt the recipe for smaller palates. For example, omit the hot sauce from a batch of chili and pass it at the table instead. Anything exceptionally bitter—like escarole—might be better left off the menu altogether.

One way to turn even a picky eater into an adventurous foodie is to involve your kids in the kitchen. When kids help cook, their willingness to eat the things you've made together soars. Outfit your kitchen with a range of tools designed for smaller hands and instill a lifelong love for cooking by enlisting them as your sous chefs. You can take this idea even further by gardening with your kids. Planting seeds and watching vegetables grow makes kids love even the least popular vegetables—like broccoli.

# ENTERTAINING

# How to Plan a Dinner Party

The simple act of inviting friends and family into one's home for a meal has somehow, during the past couple of decades, morphed from a commonplace occurrence to an event that strikes fear into the hearts of would-be hosts. Many forces are to blame for this shift, chief among them the rise of food TV. You need to see only one of the *Barefoot Contessa*'s elegant Hamptons soirees to feel hopelessly ill-equipped to host a dinner party at your place.

But you don't need a summer home or a kitchen accessory store's worth of tableware in order to invite friends to join you for a meal. Follow these simple guidelines to plan a stress-free dinner party that will make your guests—and you—happy.

1. **Crunch the numbers.** Even before you decide whom to invite, think about how many people are right for your space. How many place settings fit comfortably at your table?

Many party planning experts say that eight is the ideal number of guests at a dinner party, so if your space permits, consider taking their advice. But something smaller is equally lovely and can help build your hosting confidence.

2. **Choose the guest list.** Do you have a guest of honor, such as a birthday girl? If so, pick a mix of your shared friends and people you think she should meet. Or invite a group from a particular area of your life, for example, work friends or neighbors. Try to avoid inviting one guest who will know no one else present, especially if the rest of the group is already acquainted.

3. **Send out the invitations.** How will you ask people to come over? Options range from inappropriately informal (text message) to overkill (hand-lettered cardstock). Don't feel bad about going digital. Elegant online options exist, though there is still something extra special about getting a cute paper invite in your mailbox.

4. **Plan a menu.** Double-check what your guests can't or won't eat. A dinner party at which one guest isn't eating is awkward for everyone. Know about allergies or dietary restrictions so that you can work around them.

5. **Pick the main dish first.** Ideally, your main dish should be something you can make in advance, preferably a day or more ahead. Look to larger roasts or braised dishes—they are crowd pleasers that tend to improve after a night resting in the refrigerator.

6. **Choose the rest of your menu.** Once the entrée has been squared away, think about appetizers, side dishes, and dessert. Remember, it is not only acceptable but also advisable to take shortcuts in the form of high-quality store-bought items such as charcuterie as a starter or an impressive bakery cake for dessert. Save yourself the time and day-of stress.

7. **Clean your house.** A week before the event, pencil in a house-cleaning day on your calendar. If you do a thorough job, you'll be motivated to keep things tidy during the

intervening week, and the morning of your dinner party will require only the quickest once-over to make your space gleam again.

8. **Decide where coats go.** Especially if you live in a small space with no coat closet, you should decide in advance where coats will be stored during the party. On your made bed is a perfectly fine place. If you have a basement, a cheap clothes rack and some spare hangers might be a good investment. This step may not seem that important, but don't skip it; you'll avoid confusion when guests arrive and leave.

9. **ID all the serving ware.** You don't want to be hunting for serving bowls, platters, and utensils right as the food is ready to go to the table. Think through your menu and choose these vessels and accompanying servers in advance. Write the name of each dish on a sticky note and affix it to the appropriate serving piece. In those chaotic moments when dinner is being served, you'll be glad you did.

10. **Pick a playlist.** Choosing an evening's worth of songs can be time consuming, so do it well ahead. Think of your guests' likely tastes and choose pleasant mood music that will be more in the background than at the forefront of your party.

# How to Take a Compliment

Many people have a built-in heckler inside their brains criticizing them all the time. Psychologists refer to this as negative self-talk, and people with the most consistent and harshest inner monologues are often the least aware that it's even going on. These are the people who can't take a compliment. When something positive is said about them, they will immediately make comments refuting the praise.

When you invite others into your home, compliments come with the territory. And knowing how to politely take a positive comment is part of being a gracious host. So if you've noticed yourself deflecting, start practicing a better way to respond to your friends who will inevitably say nice things about your cooking and your home.

- **Remember that a compliment is a gift.** If you know your habit is to shoot down praise, pause for a moment when it is given and take a deep breath. Say "Thank you" just as you would if you were handed a bouquet of roses. That is the simplest and best way to take a compliment.

- **Don't refute it.** Resist the urge to tell the person that they're wrong about your home (don't say: "But it's such a mess. Don't look at the floor!") or your cooking (don't say: "Really? I thought it was overcooked").

- **Don't automatically mirror the comment.** Though you may be extremely tempted to do so, especially if you are struggling with what to say, do not volley back a compliment. You'll sound insincere. Give the person a thank-you and move on.

# What to Cook with a Kid

Children are naturally curious about what you are doing in the kitchen, and though there are definitely potential dangers you'll need to be cautious about (flames, knives, spicy foods), getting your kids involved in the preparation of family meals is a great idea. For one thing, kids are much more likely to eat stuff they helped (or even just "helped") make, especially when it comes to the healthy stuff they might otherwise turn up their small noses at. For another, you can model the meal planning and cooking skills they'll one day need. Here's how to get started.

1. **Choose a child-friendly menu.** Once you've decided to strap an apron on a youngster, you'll need to decide what to cook. Pick any dish that the child already likes that is not too complicated. Pizza and pancakes are two great choices.

2. **Teach them the rules.** If you ask them to wash their hands every time you begin, they'll be doing it without prompting before you know it.

3. **Make it fun.** Kids love kneading dough and whisking batter, and the finished short stack or slice is sure to fill them with pride and delight.

4. **Stock the right tools.** If cooking with kids is something you want to make a regular practice, invest in a set of kitchen tools designed with safety features and for small hands. You don't want to teach a child to chop with your own razor-sharp chef's knife, for example, but myriad kid-safe knives and choppers are available that allow littler chefs to peel and chop vegetables right alongside you.

# What to Cook for a Date

Cooking for someone can be very romantic. Plus it gives you a great chance to show off your kitchen skills. But cooking for a date comes with important considerations—too much of a pungent ingredient like garlic or anchovies might make you want to keep your distance from each other, and a too-heavy recipe might have you feeling sluggish after the meal.

One famous date-friendly recipe is all over the Internet: a simple but impressive roast chicken that originally appeared in *Glamour*. It's called "Engagement Chicken" because several editors at the magazine received proposals soon after making it for their beloveds. Whether or not you are ready for marriage, this lemon-and-herb-flavored recipe is a safe bet—though you'd probably be wise to avoid mentioning the recipe's name to your date. If chicken doesn't ring your bell, take inspiration from this recipe genre: classic, basic, elegant, and easy.

## Cooking *with* Your Date

If a couple is interested in food and cooking, few things make a better date than spending a day shopping for ingredients and creating a masterpiece in the kitchen together. Suggest this activity several days in advance so you can decide what to make. It should be something a bit labor-intensive and challenging—working together on a project promotes bonding and a sense of accomplishment. When you're done you can high-five, wash up, light some candles, and enjoy the fruits of your labor.

# Common Food Allergies

Food allergies are increasingly common; it's likely that you, a family member, or a friend deals with the unpleasant reality of avoiding various ingredients. When you're cooking for guests you don't know well, it's a good idea to keep in mind the most common allergens—the eight items listed on page 130. This list doesn't cover every allergy under the sun, but a full 90 percent of allergy cases involve these foods. Avoiding them isn't as daunting as it may appear. The Internet is chockablock with recipes and entire websites dedicated to cooking that is free from these ingredients.

A first step to avoiding these allergens is cooking from whole (not packaged) ingredients. Most boxed, bagged, and frozen food items contain some form of wheat or soy, for example. If you do use something from a box, scrutinize the ingredients list carefully. Some allergies are life-threatening, and exposure to even a small amount means a trip to the hospital.

The most common food allergens include:

- Peanuts
- Tree nuts
- Milk
- Egg
- Wheat
- Soy
- Fish
- Shellfish

# All about Your Home Bar

Establishing a home bar is one of the great joys of adulthood for those who like spirits and cocktails. It's your chance to choose the specific bottles, tools, and mixers that are perfectly aligned with your tastes and aesthetic. Here is some advice for organization and contents.

## The Setup

Your home bar can be located anywhere. True aficionados have been known to install full-size bars in their basement to house their collection of spirits and drinking paraphernalia, but any spare cabinet or shelf will do. Bar carts and sideboards are nice options for displaying bottles and glassware, as space and budgets allow.

# The Hardware

A successful home bar requires a few simple tools.

- **Bar spoon.** You'll need this long-handled tool for drinks that are stirred.

- **Muddler.** Essential for getting just the right flavor in many classic cocktails, including the mojito, this stick is used like a pestle to gently mash ingredients like fruits and herbs.

- **Jigger.** This measuring vessel will give you precise pours and help you follow recipes exactly. (It can also help prevent overpouring—a risk at the home bar.) The standard capacity is 1 to 2 fluid ounces.

- **Cocktail shaker.** This is for those drinks that need the hard shake.

- **Strainer.** Use it to pour drinks perfectly into glasses and removing stray bits of pulp, ice, or herbs.

- **Ice cube trays.** Get the silicone molds that

create extra-large cubes. They melt more slowly, diluting drinks less and keeping them cold longer.

- **Glasses.** You'll find a wide array of barware out there, much of it beautiful and expensive. Start with a set of six short glasses and six tall ones.

# Basic Booze

How you stock your home bar is up to you; make your own rules. If the staggering variety of liquor in the world overwhelms you, start with these five basics. Or substitute one of your favorites. Lovers of the brown spirits, for example, sometimes dedicate a home bar exclusively to whiskey and all the ways to enjoy it. Consider this list a jumping-off point.

- **Vodka.** This colorless and, ideally, flavorless spirit is the main ingredient in plenty of cocktails and a crowd-pleasing option to have handy.

- **Gin.** Essentially, this spirit is vodka flavored with herbs and spices, notably juniper. You need it to make a traditional martini and, of course, gin and tonic.

- **Whiskey.** Lots of options here. Do you like bourbon (a sweet corn-based style from the American South) or its smoky cousin from across the pond, Scotch? Maybe you prefer a spicy rye? Figure out your preferences at a bar before investing in your own bottle.

- **Tequila.** A requirement for that Cinco de Mayo staple, the margarita, tequila is distilled from the sap of the agave plant. Fans of this spirit may want to branch out into tequila's smoky sibling, mezcal.

- **Rum.** This spirit is a must-have for lovers of tropical or tiki-bar-style drinks. Light rum, which is clear, is more versatile than dark rum, which looks more like whiskey.

# Mixers

Don't go crazy stocking your bar with mixers. Choose only the ones you need to make your favorite cocktails, plus these three.

- **Triple sec.** This orange-flavored liqueur is an ingredient in many cocktails, including margaritas.

- **Vermouth.** A fortified wine, vermouth is an essential ingredient in martinis, negronis, and other classic cocktails.

- **Bitters.** Used sparingly, bitters are a kind of cocktail seasoning. You need them to make a proper old fashioned and many new-fangled drinks as well.

# Upgrades

Once you get your basic home bar in hand, you'll soon start wanting to make drinks that are even more special. Here are some ingredients that will bring your creations to the next level.

- **Amaro.** This bitter liquor is a wonderful, elegant digestive and is often used in cocktails. Campari is the most famous.

- **Chartreuse.** A green or yellow spirit from France made with brandy and herbs, it's an ingredient in obscure classic drinks that cocktail nerds love, including the Last Word.

- **Brandy or cognac.** A top-quality cognac is a delicious luxury, whether sipped on its own or mixed into a classic drink like the sidecar.

- **Freshly squeezed juices.** You can use sour mix and bottled citrus juices. Or level up your home bar with a citrus reamer, a strainer, and three minutes of effort.

- **Homemade mixers.** Get fancy by stirring up simple syrups with flavorful ingredients, like cinnamon, chili, or cucumber.

# Good Kitchen Gifts

The trouble with kitchen gifts is that the recipients often have the wrong idea about what they really need. Wedding registries are great examples. Most people do not truly need an 18-piece knife set, a bread machine, or a fancy wine decanter. Buying gifts for more experienced home cooks can be hard because cooking tools, like knives, are very personal.

Here's a list of truly good and useful gifts to consider when you want to increase someone's happiness in the kitchen, with one caveat: before buying, ask yourself if the person already has this item or if they have the space to store it in their kitchen.

- **Cookbooks.** Think of your best-loved and most-used cookbook. Buy a new copy and annotate the recipes with the valuable tips and insights you've accrued through years of cooking with it.

- **Enameled cast-iron Dutch oven.** Classic and well loved by experienced cooks, enameled cast iron tends to last for ages regardless of the manufacturer.

- **Electric knife sharpener.** Truly sharp knives are the ultimate kitchen luxury. With one of these simple machines, the perfect edge is minutes away.

- **Pressure cooker.** This is one of the absolute handiest tools people rarely buy themselves.

- **High-powered blender.** What's your budget? If money is no object, treat someone to a seriously powerful blender.

- **Cookbook stand.** This simple tool holds cookbooks upright and open so you can more easily work from the pages.

- **Gourmet goodies.** Sometimes the best kitchen gift is one you eat. You know that overpriced gelato, high-end chocolate, and sticker-shock-inducing bag of coffee beans? Buy it for someone you love. No one gets that stuff for themselves, but everyone enjoys receiving it.

- **Cooking lessons.** Hire a chef to come to their kitchen to teach a tricky dish like pad Thai or gnocchi. Or send your friend to cooking school for a night. They'll bring the new skills and tricks back to their kitchen and think of you whenever they put them to good use.

# How to Handle Red Wine Stains

Red wine stains eventually happen to everyone. Be prepared to spring into action.

1. **Salt.** This technique is particularly good for a carpet stain. Thoroughly cover the stain with salt. After several hours, vacuum the salt, and you should be looking at a vanished or at least diminished spot.

2. **Club soda.** When the spill is still fresh, pour club soda over the stain, saturating it, and then dab dry (do not rub) with a clean, absorbent cloth.

3. **Dish soap and hydrogen peroxide,** mixed together in equal amounts, can be used as a stain-fighting treatment.

4. **Try dry cleaning.** Often the pros can remove stains better than you. It's worth a try.

# Stuff We Can't Tell You

Becoming a comfortable, confident home cook is a gift you will give to yourself over time. It takes patience and practice. Eventually you'll learn:

- **How to fail.** No one learns to cook overnight. In fact, your failures will teach you infinitely more than any book. Do you have what it takes to completely screw something up, throw it away, and then start over, armed with what you've learned and a steely determination to do it right this time? Congratulate yourself for a hard-won lesson when you ruin something—you'll never make that exact mistake again.

- **How to follow your heart.** Following your culinary yens and obsessions is a must to achieve mastery over your kitchen, and indeed your food life. Heed internal cues as much as possible; go down the rabbit hole of perfecting Japanese ramen broth or cultivating a sourdough starter for bread. Some people discover their life's calling this way.

- **How to share your passion.** Ask other home cooks to show you how to do things you want to learn. As Julia Child said, "People who love to eat are always the best people." Passionate home cooks are generous and want to share. We can't tell you if you'll join our ranks one day, but we hope you do.

- **How cooking will change your life.** We *could* tell you cooking can improve your whole life, making you a better spouse, friend, or parent, making you healthier and happier, imbuing your days with the homemade magic that only your own cooking can provide . . . but you probably wouldn't believe us. At least not until you experience it yourself. Sometime, after a terrible day, you'll go to the trouble of cooking something delicious and nourishing, and as you eat it you'll realize that cooking is the bedrock of caring for yourself and others. It's the universal language of love.

- **How to be self-reliant.** We can't tell you the rebellious thrill you will get as you break from the big food companies that end up determining what most people eat. It's an exhilarating jolt of independence that only cooking for yourself can bring.

- **How to be happy in the kitchen.** Nor can we explain the shelter and sanctuary available to you right inside your own kitchen, or the fact that cooking is a kind of therapy that actually *saves* you money. One day, as you chop vegetables, you may suddenly find that a half hour has pleasantly evaporated and you don't feel burdened by the chore, but are strangely liberated by it. We can't tell you what that particular flavor of relaxed and happy feels like, but you will find it for yourself if you keep on cooking.

# Acknowledgments

Thank you to my editor, Tiffany Hill, and the inspiring team at Quirk. Thanks to my husband and first reader, Dan Call, who not only fixed a million errors but also let me steal his areas of expertise for this book—he's the cook who knows the properties of various cookware materials and how to sharpen knives. I'm also grateful to the myriad chefs, writers, bloggers, coworkers, and cooking show hosts who have made up my own unorthodox culinary school for all these years.

---

Also available:

RECIPES
Every Man Should Know

by Brett Cohen and Bryn Collins

Recipes Every Man
Should Know